Mildly Erotic Verse

The Expanded 2nd Edition

Other titles from the Emma Press

Poetry anthologies

The Emma Press Anthology of Motherhood
The Emma Press Anthology of Fatherhood
Homesickness and Exile: Poems about Longing and Belonging
Best Friends Forever: Poems on Female Friendship
Campaign in Poetry: The Emma Press Anthology of Political Poems
The Emma Press Anthology of Dance
Slow Things: Poems about Slow Things
The Emma Press Anthology of Age

Poetry anthologies for children

Falling Out of the Sky: Poems about Myths and Monsters

The Emma Press Picks

The Emmores, by Richard O'Brien
The Held and the Lost, by Kristen Roberts
Captain Love and the Five Joaquins, by John Clegg
Malkin, by Camille Ralphs
DISSOLVE to L A, by James Trevelyan (March 2016)

Poetry pamphlets

The Dead Snail Diaries, by Jamie McGarry
Rivers Wanted, by Rachel Piercey
Oils, by Stephen Sexton
Myrtle, by Ruth Wiggins
If I Lay on my Back I Saw Nothing but Naked Women,
by Jacqueline Saphra, illustrated by Mark Andrew Webber
True Tales of the Countryside, by Deborah Alma
AWOL, by John Fuller and Andrew Wynn Owen
Goose Fair Night, by Kathy Pimlott (March 2016)

MILDLY

EROTIC VERSE

Edited by Rachel Piercey and Emma Wright

With poems from Jamie Baxter, Vasiliki Albedo Bennu, Nisha Bhakoo, Julia Bird, Sophia Blackwell, Jo Brandon, Annie Brechin, Alan Buckley, Helen Clare, George David Clark, Mel Denham, Isobel Dixon, Hugh Dunkerley, Victoria Gatehouse, Mary Gilonne, Stephanie Green, Robert Hamberger, Ramona Herdman, Hilaire, Lynn Hoffman, James Horrocks, Kirsten Irving, Victoria Kennefick, Amy Key, Angela Kirby, Anja Konig, Ali Lewis, Holly Magill, Ikhda Ayuning Maharsi, Amy McCauley, Laura McKee, Fiona Moore, Steve Nash, Richard O'Brien, Camille Ralphs, Emma Reay, Kristen Roberts, Jacqueline Saphra, Lawrence Schimel, Stephen Sexton, Natalie Shaw, Di Slaney, Ruth Stacey, Jon Stone, Kelley Swain, Ali Thurm, Sara-Mae Tuson, Nicola Warwick, Ruth Wiggins and Jerrold Yam.

Illustrated by Emma Wright.

THE EMMA PRESS

THE EMMA PRESS

First published in Great Britain in 2016
by the Emma Press Ltd

This is the expanded second edition of The Emma Press Anthology of
Mildly Erotic Verse *(ISBN 978-0-9574596-2-5), which was first published
in 2013. It features 17 of the original poems in addition to 33 new poems.*

ISBN 978-1-910139-34-9

A CIP catalogue record of this book
is available from the British Library.

Printed and bound in Great Britain
by TJ International, Padstow.

The Emma Press
theemmapress.com
queries@theemmapress.com
Birmingham, UK

Contents

Foreword for Expanded 2nd Edition

When Rachel and I first started collecting mildly erotic poetry in 2013, the Emma Press was really very new and unknown. We had a decent number of submissions and were able to chose twenty-three poems which I still really love, but the resulting book – *The Emma Press Anthology of Mildly Erotic Verse* – was extremely slim, even with the extra-thick paper I cunningly had it printed on.

Our original impulse in creating the book was to showcase and celebrate the diversity of human erotic experiences, so when we reached the end of our second print run of *The Emma Press Anthology of Mildly Erotic Verse* it occurred to us that we might revisit our first bestseller and see what we could do with a few more years to our name.

Excitingly, the response to our call for submissions was so great that we were able to double the number of poems in the book, bringing extra shades (fifty?!?) of intimacy into the collection. There may now be more public discourse around desire, but I still believe – as I said in my introduction to the first edition – that society's attitude towards sex has a long way to go. I hope that the second edition of *Mildly Erotic Verse* will be a valuable contribution to this ongoing discussion.

Emma Wright
BIRMINGHAM
January 2016

Introduction to 1ˢᵗ Edition

I was pretty excited when erotic literature hit the bestseller charts in 2011. It felt like another aspect of human sexuality had entered the mainstream, as thousands of people ruled that there was nothing shameful about wanting to read about sex and different sexual practices, even in public.

But it annoyed me that many of these bestsellers weren't terribly erotic. They contained lashings of sex and were enjoyable romances, but they didn't strike me as genuinely sexy and thrilling, and I wondered if their success was contributing to the misinterpretation of "eroticism" as equivalent with "sex". This distinction between "Popular Erotica" and "Genuinely Erotic Fiction" might seem snobby or a matter of personal opinion, but when a society's attitude towards sex is still a work in progress it feels important to assert the individual identity of eroticism and understand it as a much broader, looser concept than sex, for all that they have in common.

My instinct is that eroticism exists around the edges of sex, in the anticipation and desire and in memories and associations. It exists on both cerebral and carnal levels, and it's hard to define because each person's sense of it is utterly unique. It can be wild, hilarious, beautiful and alarming; difficult to describe but the easiest thing to spot once you know what you're looking for – maybe a tiny leap in the stomach or a burst of exclamation marks in the brain.

I wanted to create a book which celebrated the diversity and eccentricity of eroticism and human sexuality, in relation to the physical aspects of sex as well as apart from it. Poetry is the ideal medium for examining elusive concepts without flattening them, and so *The Emma Press Anthology of Mildly Erotic Verse* was born.

I worried that some aspects of the brief ('mildly', 'erotic', 'verse') might deter some people, but my co-editor Rachel Piercey and I ended up collecting over 170 submissions from all over the world. The standard of submissions was high, and there were several which we liked a lot but had to let go because they didn't fit with our vision for the book. Some were more romantic than erotic; some were sexual and nothing more. There was a whole tranche of darkly erotic poems which piqued our interest but made us realise that we wanted the book to be enjoyable and encouraging, not depressing.

Which isn't to say that there are no discomfiting poems in our final selection. Quite the contrary: we wanted the anthology to skate the line between teasingly sketchy and uncomfortably raw, and I hope there are poems in this book which will surprise readers and challenge their notions of what other people – and they – find erotic. Some, like Julia Bird's *Press Play* and Kristen Roberts' *Cool change before midnight*, approach their subject from a distance, positively vibrating with restraint, while others, like Anja Konig's *Radiocarbon Dating* and Emma Reay's *Have you imagined having sex with me?* are exhilaratingly direct.

Rawness is a key part of this collection's identity, and we were conscious when selecting the poems that we wanted the book as a whole to deliver an unglossed depiction of eroticism. We wanted it to be true to the reality of adult life, which is full of mess and complications; there is space for romance and tenderness, and even the odd fairytale, but in real life erotic moments occur between the mundane and the distinctly unerotic, and are no less erotic for that. *Tight Dress*, by Amy Key, and Jon Stone's *Glamour* both examine human interactions on such an intimate level that our initial discomfort turns to awe. *Magician's Assistant*, by Richard O'Brien, takes place in a retail park and a budget hotel room; and the speaker in *To September, from June*, by Mel Denham, smells of car-exhaust while her lover dreams of caravans.

A more ambitious aim for the anthology, which goes back to my irritation with the bestselling erotic novels, was to find a new vocabulary for eroticism and sex. I feel we have reached a point where the standard phrases for evoking eroticism have lost their ability to surprise and inspire, and every stock verb, noun, adjective and adverb makes sex sound cartoonish and unappealing. Some words just need to be used more sensitively, while others should probably be laid to rest. A penis has never sounded good when throbbing, never mind the fact of being called a penis. The poets we found understood this, and among my favourite words in this anthology are new words such as *resolving, smashed, bones, spoon, moulding, trace, shallowing*; and more familiar ones like *warm, suck, stroke, wet*.

I have high hopes for this little book, which is the product of so many talented poetic imaginations. I could not be more delighted with the poems assembled inside these covers and I feel tremendously lucky to have encountered such witty, generous, insightful writers. Eroticism is alive and well in their hands.

Emma Wright
WINNERSH
July 2013

Mildly Erotic Verse

Tight Dress

I'm in the tight dress. The one that prevents dignified sitting.
The tight dress suggests I'm prepared to be undressed.
Do my thighs flash through the seams?
I try to remember if the bed is made, or unmade.
The wind is wrapping up the sound of our kissing.
I wonder should I undress first or should you undress first.
I'm not sure I can take off the dress in a way that looks good.
I consider if I should save up sex until morning.
We are far gone and I'm better at kissing when sober.
I find that your earlobes provide the current fascination.
On my bedside table are three glasses of water and my
     favourite love letter.
I try to untie your shoes in a way that is appalling.

Glamour

Beneath the boiled wool, he's just a skellybones,
and underneath the skellybones, a fumbling boy,
and underneath the boy, he's one of Jakey's twins,
and under that he's nothing but a bumblebee.
Peel back the bee and he's a coddled emperor,
and under that, she stumbles on a beery goon
but under that, none other than Hercule Poirot,
and underneath Poirot, he's just a boy again.

And she's a sweet thing underneath the stars and spurs,
a cloud beneath the sweet thing, and then under that
he finds a girl who sports a look of faint surprise,
but she too falls away and leaves a cinder smut.
The cinder smut's a cover; she's a grizzly bear
and then a toymaker and then a tomahawk,
and finally a girl who's been to Zanzibar,
a girl who thinks she might be an insomniac.

They know the thing to do tonight is sleekly slide
against each other's planes the way they do in films,
be spoon and syrup, glass and shadow, blade and blade.
But now the smell of overripeness overwhelms
the both of them, and out they slip from underneath
the glamours that had all but pinned them in their place,
two grubbied-up potato dolls with sticky breath
and all the more delighted for their ugliness.

The boy who loved welding

1.

Tipsy with clumsy-lust,
we skived the afternoon.

His overalls sweated
oil onto my office-white
shirt and the zip broke
on my new skirt.

We didn't care: threw them
to tangle their own limbs
on his bedroom floor.

It was all new to him;
not much less to me.
The single bed squeaked.
Could have sworn
I heard
ice cream van chimes.

Halfway he grabbed my hips,
bellowed a startled laugh:
'You're better than welding!'

2.

Shouldn't have done it and his mum
smirked at me, picked a bit of hay
from my hair – did I want
a cup of tea? I swallowed it,
a hot politeness new to me
but fast growing habitual;
the backs of my thighs itched
with grass seed and I gripped
the sweaty edge of their good sofa.

Avventura

Strange how giving head reminds me of Venice.
How light unzipped slow towards Murano,
a glassing of focus, that slick lap of water salting the quay.
You taught me Moon Cream Carrara, Honey Travertine,
the way veins seemed to shift as marble warmed
along those intricacies of Italian classic columns.
How to finger a basso-relievo with closed eyes,
feel the fine chiselled line between its shadowed folds,
and always use a tip of tongue to taste each grain
of caviale, before the bursting bitter swallow.

How to Kiss

LESSON 1

'D'you want me to show you how to kiss?'
I was sixteen and greedy to learn.
She was my brother's girlfriend under the moon,
standing outside a pub; the two of us
dry while he queued inside, oblivious.
It was worth the guilt. I stooped like a heron
to scoop a fish, as if breaking the skin
of water. She raised her throat, and this
moment banished feathers and scales. Her tongue
dipped briefly inside my mouth like the taste
of someone else, licked and gone.
I wanted more. My thumb stroked her wrist,
but my brother came barging out again
balancing bitter drinks to quench our thirst.

LESSON 2

'A little less tongue.' That's Patrick's advice.
I found him in the sauna, a white towel
draped over his loins; drowsy after a prowl
down dim-lit corridors where one man's face,
another man's torso, might entice.
He lazed alone inside the cubicle,
as if snoozing on an altar in a chapel,
until I hesitated, made my choice.
I stepped inside and he, by allowing me
to loosen his towel, strum the hairs on his thigh,
proved consent by the subtlest degree.
I'll do whatever Patrick tells me, try
a little less tongue tonight, softly
skim your lips with kisses where we lie.

Have you imagined having sex with me?

Have you imagined having sex with me?
Planned exactly how it would be?
Have you pictured all the faces?
The sighs, the eyes, the grimaces?
Have you schemed how we'd get started?
Am I flash-naked, legs parted?
Or maybe there's some back-story,
Of brave knights and morning glory?
Or a plumber, a pizza boy.
And what am I – coquette or coy?
Am I Russian? Or am I Thai?
With skin on thin or fat on thigh?
Am I a pliable, edible fool?
Or cougar-clawed, matured and cruel?

Do I like you? Do you hope I do?
Do you wish I were more open with you?
I might be Flora, or Fauna, or Eve, or Dawn,
Alder Trees, Laurel Leaves, Spider, Swan;
I am 5 ft. 7, fair, Caucasian;
Territory vulnerable to invasion;
I am all states; I am armies campaigning;
I am trying and taxing and waxing and waning;
I'm in orbit; I'm a film on repeat;
I'm Victory, I'm cold, I'm young, I'm defeat.
I stretch for miles, and if you tried
To run, like a stream down a mountain's side,
More faithful than you meant to be,
You could run for hours and never leave me.

Stars, Flowers, Grass and Us

After our walk in the park at dusk
I run myself a bath, hold high
the little vial: three drops of lavender.
I swirl the oil into a swift ellipse, sweet,
steaming hot, and think of how the Milky Way
is swept.   What hand stirred that?

I peel my dress up from my body's stem,
a time-lapse blossoming above my head,
arms raised a moment – praise in church –
then let the flare of fabric drop, unclip
my bra, shrug all my trappings off, step in.

As the water settles to my collarbones,
small shreds of grass release, float up:
green secret constellation drifting here
above my belly, ribs, small watery shadows
cast upon my skin.   Now there's no doubt
whose hands it is I'm thinking of.

A well–tempered keyboard

Now that I am finally getting laid again
my piano playing is improving. What else
would I do in those moments of waiting
bathed, perfumed, satinned, variously
analgised and anaesthetised?

It seems impossible to me now, that
anyone could play Bach without thinking
of sex. More than the insistence of that
pulsing left hand chord, it's the way we move
from key to key as if harmony were a body.

My fingers are getting nimbler; I can dream
of grace in those quick passages, almost
believe that nerves could heal. I've noticed too
that these days sex ends like a chorale, a single
note slipping into the home chord: a-a-men.

Phosphorescence

Record this you say and I'm left
in the shallows, holding your phone.

And I capture it all – the moon
low and lush as a forbidden fruit,

you, striking light after light
as you cross the bay, the way

your face, as you turn to wave,
is star-varnished like that of a god.

Before you upload, before the flurry
of *likes* for this phenomenon,

there's a moment when your world
is gleaming in my hands. Tonight

I would gulp down this blooming ocean
for a taste of your skin.

The Gift

I knew then, if I hadn't known before –
seeing you at that hippie bash in pink,
drawn to the rolling strut and thrust of your
tight hipsters, glancing at the strip of skin
under the shrunk-down tee – how anyone
might have that shock, as feelings pressure up
from some persistent spring, thought to be long
dried out. I squeezed my arms into the hug
and sensed your breath, its feather on my neck.
There was no shame. We both knew some things live
quite happily in shadow, and unsaid,
their insubstantiality their gift.
We eyed the women, did the weigh-up talk;
the way men do, like sparring Bantam cocks.

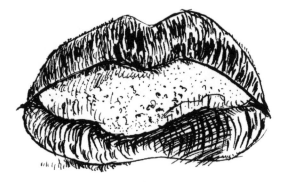

Pinkie Minimus

I asked you to keep the promise
using your, my Pinkie Minimus,
like when we were children.

I hoped that you would keep your promise
that we made by Pinkie Minimus
like when we were moppets.

But what did you do
but suck my Pinkie Minimus,
wrestled with worms and germs.

Yes o yes o
my Pinkie Minimus
has been sucked,
licked by your blunt tongue.
O no o no no
what I asked was the promise
of lost childhood,
two Pinkie Minimus
linked to each other.

Yes o yes o
we should have put our wedding rings
on the tiny
platoon
Pinkie Minimus.

Shave

The backs of men's necks
queue on the Tube.
Hot breath and the mustn't
of reaching to touch. Such
a little inch of shared air
to transgress. Sticky dress
and long haul home to owned skin.

When I was eighteen,
my lover asked me to stand over him
with little buzzing clippers, to stroke
the hair off with their insect mouth.
I kissed all up that new tickle
of conquered skull, triumphant.
He walked beside me shorn, marked mine.
My thumb the first to smooth across, enjoy
the bite of new-cut hair.

Another summer, older,
and it's my father asking.
Widower, too ill to go out.
Such uncomfortable trespass,
shudder and prickle,
to walk the clippers the way his second wife did,
cut paths over his small grey head.
I swept up after. I holstered the clippers
in the leatherette case and put them away
in the too-tidy bathroom of his last house.

———————

There will always be another summer.
This one, both of us in this dappled, dazzling bath,
I rest one heel
                      then the other
on your shoulder, lean back
and trust your razor
down my leg, nuzzling
the unseen back of my knee.

The Globemakers

We've been in bed all day. The winter sun
has nudged its pale head at our bedroom window
but, with no audience, has quickly gone.

I'm moulding the warm spheres of you, my hands
softly holding your skull's stubborn curve,
ticking with life, all your well-loved lands

elaborately renamed. Knees, elbows, hips
become meridian, terrain, equator,
the plains between them measured by my lips.

We know the world, its inkblots and crevasses,
its latitudes. The stars are where we left them.
We know the streets, their gutters, their sadness,

but these four hands are artful instruments
that can remake a world, and these warm sheets
are full of fallen rivers and lost crescents

of moon and paper. So we pinch them tight
between our fingers, paste them into place.
Something stirs, an extra inch of light

shimmering closer, ice becoming water,
something beyond the sea-wall of the night
that's vigorous, and sweet, and isn't winter.

My Love, the Shetland Trowie

After Rabelais

His eyes are like extinguished lighthouses
His eyebrows are a gadderie of fiddlers
His nose a broken sea-arch
His jaw is like the blue ramp of the ferry lowering
                then clanking shut
His mouth a hollow gloup
His teeth smashed Blue Vodka bottles
His saliva is like the seven tides of Shetland
His chest hair a scratchy kishie
His arms whirling wind turbines
His elbows are like crane-winches
His legs are posts bristling with barnacles
His buttocks are half-submerged skerries
His member is like the seal's head bobbing up
                and down in the harbour
His bollocks are ponies' nose-bags
His pubic hair is the hay-nets flung
                over plastic rubbish bags
His arsehole is like the slippery steps down
                to the lower deck
His piss is the swell in a Force 10 gale
His sweat is salty houb water
His oxters are like skories' nests
His nipples are the rings of salmon-traps
His navel is a fire-bucket peppered
                with fag butts

His skin is like stiff, sea-drenched gaiters
His breath's a blow-hole
His sigh the haar
His fart is like the flare at Sullom Voe

Glossary: *gadderie* – gathering; *gloup* – collapsed cave; *haar*
– sea-mist; *houb* – salty loch; *kishie* – woven straw pannier;
oxter – arm-pit; *skorie* – adolescent herring gull; *trow* or *trowie*
– Shetland troll.

Hare

for Bethan

*

> *Snakes that cast your coats for new,*
> *Chameleons that alter hue,*
> *Hares that yearly sexes change.*
> – Fletcher, *The Faithful Shepherdess*

I

You were surprised by its huge ears,
alert and stiff in the long grass

its masculine nose,
the lithe terrier-like body.

We were almost on it
when the hare erupted into flight

something more like a deer
than a rabbit in the way it ran

bounding in fast surefooted leaps
across the astonished field

until it veered suddenly, rose into the air
and was gone in the dusk of the wood

leaving only this impression
warm in the still unravelling grass.

II

Warm in the still unravelling sheets,
I run my fingers down your spine

trace the soft vestigial hair of an animal
that only minutes ago I held

bucking in my arms, a fierceness
I'd never imagined, straining for release

a changeling that slipped between my fingers
and was gone with a cry

now resolving itself back into you.

Office hour

in his dim, cluttered room
and he's going over the derivation
of Spearman's correlation coefficient but I
am correlating to the coefficient of his ring finger,
taken by the girth of the wrist flexor packing
his unbuttoned cuff. I am close
enough to see the warp
of his poplin shirt, breathe in the woody
base note of his aftershave. And now
a message pops up on his screen, something
about the tightness of duct tape on
lips and a whip, and all I can do
is pretend I didn't see,
but I did. But I did.

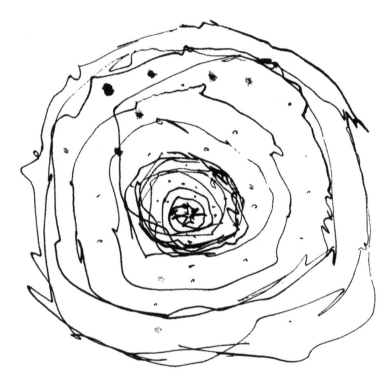

He liked her to talk about other women's breasts

Bridget's nipples are small and pink,
tiny strawberries she offers to her baby.

Eva's breasts: round like puddings
whipped and creamy, pale, freckled –

then Sam, always on display,
flat as Marie-Antoinette's

champagne cups – pop! And then the fizz
(her head – her head quite gone by then)

Contagion

In the lecture theatre, I sit in the dark
    (there will be slides about Visigoths).
You stroll in: odour of unwashed socks and Lynx
    invades, sticks
to this plaid shirt which I wear
    in an ironic way, breasts
push against the check,
    strain blue-flecked buttons.

You wear a sweater

big and woolly, with sleeves that go way past your hands –
    if I ever see your hands,
if I catch one glimpse I will lick them, palm to thumb,
    suck
        each
            finger.

You sit in front of me, my pupils expand,
    you have a cold, one that needs a tissue –
a couple of tissues, a full, glorious box, but you don't have any,
    you messy thing.
You use your sleeves, *you use your*
    sleeves, you sneeze and I wish I knew your name.
I mumble 'Goth Bless you', hope you'll hear,
    you run your sweet nose over a loose cuff.

I wear this plaid shirt

I want to rip to pieces, let puny buttons fall in surrender,
    as spoils of Visigoth pillage project on the white screen
in Boole Basement Lecture Theatre One, I want to
    blow

        your

            nose.

how we taste

we once had a map
and thought we knew

where to unbury the salty
and the sweet

then we discovered
these buds spread wider

saliva wets the folds of things
and pours

into the whole of our mouths
and down our throats

touches nerves in our heads
teaches our tongues to crave

Prize

Like a swig of medicine, the undressing is easy;
I watch the sun rehearse over the arena,
its lonely eye laying mahogany sheets
on a row of strangers. Then, when it rages
enough for a change, I slip
soundlessly in the pool, legs
pivoting for the kick-off, as if recalling the force with
which a man enters my quiet chamber. And the sun
agrees, setting live wires over a turquoise floor;
I am drawn to its audacity, its electrical charm
tamed by water. Later in the changing
room we would smile, just short of crime, desperation
stiffening like a drug as we become
conjoined, at the pelvis, every breath
also traced with time's impatient handwriting.
It ends as it may only end, wrenched
free to false safety, as if afraid
of intimacy. I press a finger
to the slag, to my lips,
its awkward musk
stinging like genius. By then
you would have gone, so sure of
diving into another life.

Their letters

1st May 1610

Her letter

is pressed from flour-damp breast to Judas-hand Joanna,
hides in spinster folds to pass the Hall, makes its way first
to lips then nose, Peter eager for the hard-worked scent of
her, his Rose with lush, wide petals and soft sticky buds,
last pinched and tipped on Hollyn Hill St George's Day
past, under the crab apple and in sudden view of big John
Beale, his face a ruddy fluster, his mouth a sour bene-
diction recocked to testimony after. Her letter brings an
intake of delight, a crotch twitch of sweet slickness full re-
membered, invites him to visit her indoors, her husband
Nicholas off to Lincoln at short call, her window open 10
o'clock this night, and she will take him in.

6th May 1610

His letter

travels safe to Bilsthorpe with trusted Thomas, firm
downward strokes on stiff white parchment vowing more
than she could dream, trapped in this loveless for six cold
years, her husband good for canny trade everywhere except
in bed, a man of stolid hopes and shuttered heart. His
letter teases with dotted i's and double crossed t's, flushes
hot tongue thoughts of curls and thighs until her forehead
pounds, leant hard against the larder door. His letter pleads

she risk again, to meet him outside her house tonight
when the moon turns away so not to be complicit in their
sin. His letter in its supple roll enfolds their last two near
escapes and tightens them to nothing, her sweaty fingers
toying with the ribbon, willing to believe.

11th July 1610

Her husband's statement

is a blackened growl of grudged restraint, a tamping down
of what would be invective if the form had given room,
if the Magister had asked for more than fact, more than
witnesses had proffered as they lined to spew their sordids
into village rumour pots. Her husband's statement tells he
found their letters (the shame), had them followed (the
scandal), offered battle for his name (the honour), turned
down money for his wife (the strumpet), would not coun-
tenance divorce (the defeat). Her husband's statement
spikes the good brown paper with each ink jab, though
why the scribe is angered by dictation lies unrecorded.
Her husband never learned to read or write, guessed
instead their letters meant no good, hidden as they were
inside the corn crock, smeared by too much touching, her
round, white body heat, the smell of inner thigh when she
wore them like a trophy beneath her skirts.

The Frozen Man

At the cusp of the year in absolute dark
    she calls his name. She catches
        scatters of him in the soft cup of her hands
           until he is too much to hold. He falls
              and falls, until he covers the bed.

Slowly, she breathes him into warmth,
    her pink tongue patient against
        his white-blue beauty,
           her body moulding him,
              her legs embracing him.

She knows his coldness will not keep;
        before the spring, he will melt
           complete from her hands.

Yours truly, Stephen Dedalus

…the long foul letters he had written in the joy of guilty
confession and carried secretly for days and days…
> – James Joyce, *A Portrait of the Artist as a Young Man*

Another naked Sunday here is pillowed
on a sigh. Here lies the idea of your soft knot
of knee, that thigh honeyed in light and blazing
on the bed; here lies this beating fist. Here,

lies. And saturated in your gasp even on this
a dry night, the sky rolling away like the white
of your eyes… I've felt your body shimmer
                on my skin like dawn

on a waterlogged meadow, your hot breath
floating freckles from my cheek. Or I have
dreamt it, and felt so, so sorry. I fear I maybe
                loved it more than God.

_____

And but forgive me – me and every cowson
just like me and every scarf of kisses I knit
nightly for your neck (you mustn't know this).
I am wanting. But forgive. For if I could,

I'd fumblemouth your name into absurdity
with love of saying it. I'd serve, turn over
more hours in learning your face than if
                            these hands were clock-hands.

But throw this in the fire. Too much said, too
much turmoiled in blood. And much too young.
I Matthew 19:4. I hate to love you more. I beg
                            you don't reread this.

The Student

It's 7am in the park. You're pretending
you don't see the grime-chested kendo student
drilling, *hakama* stretched into a theatre,
bokken now passing like a wing before him.
His forearms and fingers are lean, and you're feeling
his weight on your own and his hands on your wrists.
He brings down the sword with a shift of his hips.
Advances, quite cat-like, fresh sweat on a forelock.
Tonight you'll draw ronin in *hicho* like herons.
Tonight you'll be dreaming of jostling red fish.

Helen of Troy in the Bath

There's an old claw-foot, blue, with brass taps.
The handles fall off when I turn them.
But enough hot water to shame a mortal in this age of austerity.

I add bubbles.
I like my wine almost black, tasting of ashes,
a cremation of grapes.

Disrobing, I slide in. Flush pink, hands and feet screaming.
Why the British keep their homes so cold, I'll never understand.
Your climate fosters a morbid disposition.
Melancholia. Poetry.

'Fathomed'. It's a good word.
Though when it comes down to the act,
a woman wants to be made love to, or fucked.

I run my hands over my breasts, fathoming.
It's the sort of tub for fathoms.

Conjuring forty toy ships, I let them float.
They'll founder near the islands of my thighs.
Perhaps every man yearns to be Odysseus.
Then despite it all, his marriage wouldn't run aground.

The tap chokes. What is it we wish to comprehend?
Love? Everyone always writes and rewrites
the story of my mother. We can see there's enough lust
to go around, but not where one needs it.

For heaven's sake, my ancestors were screwing geese.
Swans.

Tell Mephistopheles I'll magick my own illusions:
like these ships, listing in my coils of hair –
and all those tiny souls on board.

I take up a razor, warm it in the hot water.
Sometimes it's pinfeathers the blade scrapes
from my legs and underarms. Don't tell.
I'd say they're white as snow, but I could be lying.

The wine, the bubbles, make me giddy:
I'll pull the plug, watch my forty ships
spiral, and spiral,
                    and spiral down the drain.

Radiocarbon Dating

It's no longer done,
comparing a woman's body to a landscape –
buttock hillocks, dales and deltas –

politically incorrect. But I want you
in charge of manning up an expedition to undefined
white spaces on my map. I want you

to use your scientific training, evaluate
my forestation, measure the circumference of both
polar caps. You can examine drilling cores

to reconstruct my seismic history. The positions
of tectonic faults, degree of liquefaction
of the crust and mantle imply

tremors are possible and could be more
than model settlements can handle.

You can still shift your paradigm, embrace
a post-colonial sentiment and keep your footprint light.

Fairy Tale

Lying naked atop the sheets in the summer heat
his lumpy genitals press against his crotch
like a frog crouched
in the thick reeds of dark pubic hair.

'Kiss me,' they whisper
'and I shall grow into a prince.'

The best lovers

don't want to marry, they don't want children
or to settle down. They lay you

on a mattress in a room full of mirrors
and turn the switch to pitch black.

They drive you to an orange grove
in October. They leave faint

blossom on your skin.

Years later you will see their photographs
in exhibitions and remember

how the midday fell through their skylight,
how they brewed you fresh coffee,

how your fingers tore
their sheet apart and your back

arched like a question mark.

the jackal and the moon

give me your hand, he says,
jonquil eyes suspended by drink;
tightrope quick, he lurches towards
the doom of her red lips.

she smiles, unfurling her tiny paw,
with an arch look asks:
will you read it?
smacking her lips suggestively
like a jackal inhaling the steam
from the entrails of a kill
on a cold night.

I see a hand, he intones,
beginning the assault
with a flick of his tongue
in the centre of her palm.
a soft hand...

softer than other hands?
she is very dangerous in this light,
the cool, white sheen of her cheeks glowing.
no better, he says. *no worse.*
and your eyes...

no better? she waits,
breath bated.
your left eye being somewhat higher, perhaps...
he considers, head tipped with whimsy.

her eyebrows bristle,
flecks of gold ignite in her eyes.

your neck...
she clasps it protectively,
the five jewels of her fingertips
flexing possessively.
... as much like a neck as I have ever seen.

she hardens her heart, snaps
who do you think you are?
her white teeth cracking together,

a movie clapboard
proclaiming: *The End!*
she begins to turn away, hungry for other meat.

oh, but Biatista, he squeezes her palm.

*I could make you howl
against the blood-soaked moon,
till the juices of our bodies overran ourselves.
if you smashed yourself against me,
I'd strip you like a taxidermist
strips a dead animal,*

*till the you you were was a husk
and the you you are is coated in musk,
thick as peanut butter,
straight from the jar...*

what's the matter with you?

don't you know how to talk to a lady?
her arch twang inhabits curiosity like an old fur coat,
as she purrs along his neckline, watching his pulse.

he thinks of how he'd like to bite
the virgin flesh of her clavicle,

sink his teeth into soft skin,
worrying at her woman's bones.

oh Biatista, you know I never lie,
your eye is an eye.
your hair, like hair anywhere.
but come with me
and we'll be good together,
that I guarantee.

Biatista gave a smile
which cut through his ribs
like a prison shiv,
curled up her claws and...
came to him.

and the night was a night,
and the moon was a moon as bright
as the moon is wont to be,
and that's alright,
that's just as it should be.

Maine Man

Your shoulders are smooth
as the cool water of Long Pond
when we swam there last summer,
slippery beneath my fingers
like that solitary boulder
which you told me was erotic,
and since then I have liked to think
of it squatting there beside the lake,
alone but sure of itself and proud
of its sex appeal – so why tell me now,
amongst so many other things
I would rather not know,
that you'd really said erratic?

Down the Aisle

As the gold band slid over,
her vena amoris throbbed.

Each throb was a naked limb,
a flaunting of ceremony –

even as her finger became a full stomach
against a slender girdle,

delicious thoughts roared through her blood,

a euphemism
for where they really made noise.

The ring tightened – each urge
made her finger swell, the vein

protruded, a hernia of desire, a violaceous pulsing
that stripped even the priest of his senses.

Congregation was not divided by bride and groom
but by those who recognised her ailment

and those who pretended they did not.

Bananaphagy

He peels the skin part way back –
three flaps drooping
like a luscious tropical flower
trumpeting its stamen.

She skins the thing completely –
no messing, just brute exposure
of the fruit, holding it bare
in her fingers, a squidgy boomerang.

The dirty deed itself is done
behind each other's backs. Some acts
are best imagined. The greedy gobble,
the slo-mo chewing down to pulp.

Their afterglow – a pair of empty sacks,
bedding down together, making sweet compost.

Come With Me

After, sloth-like with satisfaction,
bed covers on the floor and panting,
we smile and ask: where were you?

Versailles: gold bed posts with raspberry
corset and cloud-white stocking ruffles,
you were a rakish courtier – and you?

Victorian attic: iron bed frame,
eager water flicking the window pane,
you were the sharp-eyed maid – and you?

Yurt: thick with clinging incense, the sound
of ponies stamping, bows and arrows,
you were a bold, fierce warrior – and you?

Japanese garden: bright running stream,
maple leaves falling, painted skin,
you were the Geisha kneeling – and you?

Mountain air: fir trees and snow peaks,
creak of leather boots and eagle shriek,
you the lone-wolf in a cabin – and you?

Casserole

As if you wouldn't feature in every one
of my slow-baked plans – you conspicuous
as parakeets that fill my north/south sky
in flocks of hopeful green.

I wouldn't eat your casserole unless
you said to. You wear dark green on lightest
pink, autumnal scarves. Let's disappear
in Wiltshire – you'll put those socks on

and I'll take them off. I think maybe
it *is* the mascara, but then again no –
leaves turn you rich with gifted colours.

Out walking then home 'to read', I'll pop
your wellies off like corks. You put enough
wood in the burner to last us all night.

Cool change before midnight

At ten we open the windows
and the cool air rolls in like a tide,
soothes the heat-sullen rooms
and settles the kids
in their sheet-tangled thrashing.

We shower in darkness
as though light itself holds warmth,
the water dancing on our skin
as the sour graffiti of the day streams away
and the relief of night unfurls.

Naked we run through the house,
flick our hair at each other
and feel the startling kiss of droplets
on flesh that's too seldom bare,
and trace their sliding trails with our tongues
under the pale eye of the moon.

To September, from June

I am already mythologising.
Maybe that's why I invoke a Greek hero's quest
as we descend the steep stairs
to a Smith Street streaked with late-night rain

In your version of heaven you live in a caravan by the sea
In mine there's a city apartment
a decorous distance from your
untrustworthy hands

We would meet
but not too often
having had plenty of practice caressing
the palpable texture of absence

In my dim-lit room cluttered
with books I would taste
salt on your lips

On your sheets we'd dishevelled
within earshot of the moan and sigh
of waves you'd bury
your face in my hair's faint
car-exhaust scent

Don't let me get too old you say as if
I can stop time like you
kill speech when you put your mouth to mine – *Oh
loosen the tongues of my mute body*

In place of that paradise on which the sun may never rise
know this instead:
tonight when your familiar voice
speaks and your familiar hand
moves

it's a present
pleasure I can't grasp to keep
my own hand
table-bound and calm
the clamour from my – *take me* – traitorous heart.

Birch

Prostrate birch –
what's with all the reaching?

So keen for something
that you can't get straight.

You lean. Invite me to
saddle up. Strong-backed

you speak to me
in mushroom and lichen.

Go on,
green my tongue.

Critical Reading

When you breathe 'Lead me into the woods'
I trace a breadcrumb trail down the flood
of your back, dropping two coin kisses
in the shallow hollows at the base.

When you purr 'What's the time Mr Wolf?'
I unravel a woodsman scar, rolling
a claw from clavicle to navel,
following the fault line with pointed tongue.

When you beg 'Show me the lands in the sky'
I spread beanstalk tendrils from the curve
of your calves, grazing ever upwards
to the gentle hum of fee – fi – fo – fum.

When you call out 'Mirror, show me the future'
I press a promise from my lips to yours:
no matter the vision your emerald eyes see,
the reflection in mine is all that you need.

But when you scream 'Shuck me like an oyster!'
I wish you came with appendices.

Rhyming Rita and Silver Sam

Rhyming Rita's watching Silver Sam –
she likes to watch the old man's muscles,
vines, she says, smaller harvest, sweeter fruit.
She's couched just so, a pillow here
a cushion there. He walks slowly, naked,
smiling as if time were no thing at all.
(Sammy knows about time, seen his share,
likes it every way but empty.)
He kneels and draws the lines of Venus lightly
with his fingers, skating figures on her warm skin.
She gathers him in, he fits just so you know.
He kisses lips and neck and breasts and belly,
he's an avalanche, our Silver Sam,
down Rhyming Rita mountain.
At the base, at the very thinness of
her thicket, he brushes the brush and whispers
away and talks in tongues, his story starting
slow, tilted, sideways, soft, barely there –
then only there where there there
'No, go, slow, slow, oh, go, go'
says Rhyming Rita as Sam delays and plays
in all the ways he knows.

It's later, she's lost count, he never started.
Rhyming Rita starts to cry,
'Oh my oh why,
I hate this fate, so late, so late,
so wrong it took so long

to find you' and Sammy says
'It's not so late,
and slow beats fast,
we only saved the best for last.'

Press Play

I

Load too much credit in the jukebox
    and every single ever written
        starts to play at once.

Vocals and bass lines,
    choruses and middle eights,
        session brass, children's choirs, sitars

swept up in a high tide of soundwaves
    lining up and clicking home
        and wiping themselves out.

The composite hit
    is a white wall of sound.
        Decibels unreadable as silence.

II

Replay and overlay us the last time
    with every time that's gone before.
        You, me, and. You, me, or.

Touch is papered over touch
    like a ricked joint rubbed numb,
        or gooseflesh on sunburn.

Like a stack of transparencies
    held to the light, such
        chaotic couplings –

a pinned or stretching limb
    in every second of a circle, some
        bomb blast or star burst. Some chrysanthemum.

III

With the white noise on repeat,
    attune yourself till every cell
        buzzes like a snare drum

and pick them out:
    that run of double claps,
        Minnie's head-notes, shattering.

A low sliding scale of Tom,
    and the song that holds its nerve
        on the fadeout rainstorm.

The Horse of My Love

I led the horse of my love to the wood
and tethered it there. And when the autumn came,
its reins fell like dead leaves shivering downwards.

Its coat took on the colours of the trees.
I slipped the bit from the gentle of its mouth
and loved it all the more.

As the season changed, I found a forest pool,
knelt and lapped the chill of water,
refreshed my mind with ice-melt.

I cupped a little in my hand, carried it
through the crackled grass to my home
and washed my face.

Icewater pulsed in my veins.
I knew, then, I needed to be warmed
to make me human.

This desire forced me out into a night
of misted breath and solitude.
My stomach growled in emptiness.

It pushed me to where my little love was stabled,
quiet as a winter's eve. I fed the horse of my love
on red apples till my hands were sore with juice.

photographs from our holiday in bed

this is
   the night we slept how you draw an x in maths
   the night we lay facedown smug as pocket aces
   the night we peeled apart like pitta from itself
   the night I was ampersand and you were treble clef
   the night we were paper figures strung across the bed
   the night our bodies framed a question asked in Spanish
   the night you coiled yourself into a burning ear
   the night you unravelled like a Danish or a fern
   the night we were the 't's in 'better'
   the night that I was seat and seatbelt
   the night that you were cloak and brooch
   the night that I was scarf and snowshoes
   the night we slept like harboured boats
   the night we were coil and core of a magnet
   the night we were strawberry and lime in a Twister
   the night our hips were a painting of hills
   the night we slept like the logo of Kappa
   the night we were stacked like strata in clay
   the night the bed wore its sheet off the shoulder
   the night you led from your hand to mine
   the nights we fashioned from day

I Went to a Parthenogenesis Party and Met an Aphid

I jerk you off
a rose, with my hand
moving as if to unsheathe
a sword.

Your body is
a chamber of nymphs,
my Russian Dolly.

Sap sucked,
six of you
dropped onto me.

We lay there
in stillness,
we were
clones of each other.

A ladybird
arose, shedding
spotted clothes off
her shoulders.

I see her split
down the middle
like her name.

You turned green
as she came
for her prey.

You left me.
None of you
can know
how to be alone.

Bluebells

are glowing under the birch trees.
The sign says Do not pick the flowers.

But I want their cold flesh
in my hands – to pick
and pick, until juice runs down
the inner sides of my wrists.

His long back, long feet
are covered in gold hair.
It's the wolf of course.
What he wants from me is unspeakable
they said.

Bluebell sap has soaked my skirt.
His paws are soft. His mouth is hot –
his breath steams,
smells of bilberries, brambles.
They lied about the meat.

I'll show you the way he says.
I don't want to hurt you.

The cottage door is open –
a smell of earth, fallen leaves.
I take off my coat and go upstairs.

Mad flash

Your face is on fire
as you take in my raven
moist and cake
naughty behind curtains
gold curtains have eased
the heart that pumps for itself
alone, loose and paw-pink
flushing the organ of cartoon
beats and bruises I received from
the tentacles of neighbours
(they never put glass in their eyes)
feeling me up, fastening
to my venison thighs
stripping me like a pin-up
whipping the dream of pill-white skin
burning my breasts with Velcro palms
arousing me with the sharps of
their nails
chicken scratch surface
chicken scratch strips
walk away, your dog is barking
pull up your socks
I know all about your eyes
can't you see I'm ready to liquefy?
your face is on fire your face is on fire.

Second Circle

We were alone, and we suspected nothing.
— Dante Alighieri (trans Mandelbaum)

You've been going through each book and CD.
I've found the long black threads of your hair
in *Crash*, which you aren't ashamed to read aloud.

So with the wind as it is, yes, there
is a case for staying the night; branches
twist and slap at the picture window – where

I'll draw the blind – submitting evidence.
The streetlights have remade
the pressing oak trees into silhouettes.

All this in the wind makes a house of my bed.
The wind insists. The wind
is your breath shallowing on the back of my head.

I wake in the night with you behind
me and the wind slight at the window sill.
One twig
            scratching an inch of glass reminds me

you are not asleep
                        your hands are far from still.

Magician's Assistant

Legs. Released by the entrance song
they spread like an accordion,
collapse. I have been working on

resistance to your charms –
and failing that, my upper arms.
Dry ice evades all smoke alarms.

*

After the show I hold your cloak
above the dust of the retail park.
Step lightly, darling, through the dark.

Your sequined foot unsticks the clutch;
unchoreographed, our belts click shut.
An escapologist is never stuck.

One room. You clatter through the minibar;
your wrists, their first-time fire-thrower scars.
My heart's a sleeve that won't stop spilling scarves.

*

I'm breathless at your sleight of hand;
be good to me, the Great, the Grand.
The cushions levitate. I never see them land.

We climb inside your velvet trunk,
dodge hidden drawers, gewgaws and junk,
half-dressed and more than halfway drunk,

and bring the lid down, plush with galaxies
that stroke your spine, lending their light to me.
I'm finding glitter in your hair for weeks.

*

Another town. You spin the box
then come toward me, blade aloft,
brushing my fingers when you turn the locks.

I curl my knees up, count to ten
and let you split me, put me back again.
Exhale. I was a different person then.

Auto-Pornographia

You and I, little lovebud,
have not always been well-acquainted.
        Out of sight, out of mind.

Come then, little extraneous,
from your stable of folds.
Sing your song of terminal neglect,
terminal longing.
        You had such hopes, bud.

Come to my right hand,
little useless. Swell
under the thumb and spread
your tiny fleshwings.
        O illicit finger buffet.
        O snaffled peripheral bloom.
Pour draught upon draught
        of glitter across my skin.

I will give in, wee harlot,
to the slutty Mexican wave. I will bite
down on the dried up gag.
        O underused one.
        O surplus to the body's economy –

Come, I will sing you this song
        that I make with my right hand.

Cigarettes

It's August, hot, and a newly-married
couple in Mobile have left the window
partly open to the night and road noise
while they make love on a futon in the dark.
After, as he breathes heavy on the pillow
beside her and a thin clear string of semen
seems to quiver on the white guitar
that is her belly, she sighs and says,
Oh, now I wish I had a cigarette.

He's been thinking he should pull the sheet
from where it's bunched along the floor
and it takes him a moment to understand
that cigarettes – which both of them detest
and she has never tried – are not her point.
She phrases it that way because pleasure
is complicated, more so perhaps than suffering.
It will augment and diminish, both,
not unlike the ancient priests who'd purge
the humid entrails of the pharaohs
and then bathe the bodies' cavities
with myrrh and frankincense and palm wine,
freights of fragrance in the hollows after.
She means that monuments to rapture
should be light to carry and combustible,
toxic in small quantities even secondhand,
and with an odour that darkens one's clothes.

Somehow he comprehends this vaguely.
It reminds him of a concert he attended
in high school, the massive outdoor stage
where the band played one encore, a second,
then mangled their guitars across the amps
and footlights: sparks, debris, electric howling.
Stoned and riding home with his ears fuzzing
in the back of a friend's Topaz, he felt
invincible and fantasized a car crash.
He'd passed out then, and later, coming to
sore-throated and coughing on his parents' porch
where the guys had left him, it was as though
some breakneck song – all glass and metal
in his mind – had wrecked around him.
He rose there slowly and limped out of it
the way a man emerges from a shattered
windshield, the live adrenaline already
funneling off, but with a few stray echoes
still looping through his chest like feedback.

Tonight on the far side of the room
the infinite lungs of the wall clock exhale
long gray minutes. Eyes shut, motionless,
his wife leans toward sleep. Her teeth
are tingling faintly, white but crooked
on the bottom row. She has clenched
and ground them during sex again
and now she guesses at the likelihood
of braces in her future when there's money.
It is her habit to sweep the tender downside

of her tongue across the misalignments
where the frets of wire might someday run,
and for a moment her mouth becomes
the smoky back room in a downtown bar
where a struggling band from out-of-state
is just about to plug in their Les Pauls.
Nascent music crackles in the outlets,
jittering, almost perceptibly, the ashtrays.

A breeze sleepwalks the curtains back
into the room and out again. Back and out.
Her husband slides his heel along her calf
and starts to tell her they should set his legs
on fire (she could inhale while they kiss),
but no, she's gone unconscious. Instead,
he pulls the sheet to their shoulders
and thinks, as he dissolves beside her, how
from a distance they would look like two
thin cylinders wrapped in white, their minds
these grainy filters in their heads. Asleep
before he gets to who might smoke them
and why, his breathing slows and deepens.
The room cools slightly. The traffic
lulls outside and the sex aroma dissipates
till only the air that cycles through their chests
is warmed and sonorous and redolent.

Layers

It's hot in here after the snow.
           I don't feel it
      until we've hung our jackets
                on chair backs,
      unloaded lunch from trays
and sat down. Then I
               pull my thick jersey off,
                  up over my head.
As I push back some
               flying hair
      I half-see, half-sense
your reaction:
             a sort of tenderness,
      amused and even
               bemused,
which makes me
      aware of myself,
                  aware that all I want to do is
strip for you
      now
      and press my whole length
               close against yours.

Did you sense this
             when I turned away
      to fold the jersey?
             Maybe you did, but
it is more beautiful
             not to know.

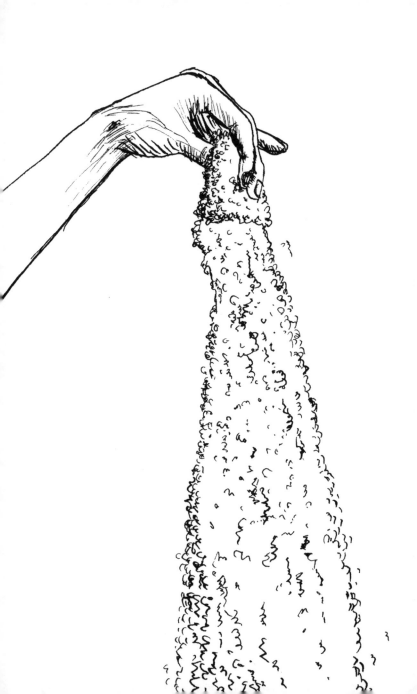

Acknowledgements

Acknowledgements and thanks are due to the original editors and publishers of some of the poems in this anthology:

'Tight Dress', by Amy Key, was first published in her debut pamphlet, *Instead of Stars* (tall-lighthouse, 2009).

'How to Kiss', by Robert Hamberger, was first published in *The North* 52 (Spring 2014).

'Stars, Flowers, Grass and Us', by Isobel Dixon, was first published in *The Dark Horse* 32, Spring and Summer 2014.

'The Gift', by Alan Buckley, was first published in *Magma* 37, Spring 2007.

'Shave', by Ramona Herdman, was first published in *The North* 53, Autumn 2014, and on *Ink, Sweat and Tears* in 2015.

A version of 'My Love, the Shetland Trowie', by Stephanie Green, was first published in her pamphlet *Flout* (HappenStance, 2015).

'Hare', by Hugh Dunkerley, was previously published in *Irish Pages* 4.1 and his collection *Hare* (Cinnamon Press, 2010).

'He liked her to talk about other women's breasts', by Natalie Shaw, was first published in *Butcher's Dog* 4 (Autumn 2014).

'how we taste', by Laura McKee, was first published in *The Journal* in 2015.

An earlier version of 'Prize', by Jerrold Yam, was first published in *Scattered Vertebrae* (Math Paper Press, 2013).

'Their letters', by Di Slaney, was previously published in *The Interpreter's House* 58 and on the Poetry School CAMPUS blog.

'Helen of Troy in the Bath', by Kelley Swain, was previously published in *Atlantic* (Cinnamon Press, 2014).

'Fairy Tale', by Lawrence Schimel, first appeared in *Deleted Names* (A Midsummer Night's Press, 2013).

'the jackal and the moon', by Sara-Mae Tuson, was first published in the *Loose Muse* anthology (2012).

'Maine Man', by Angela Kirby, was first published in her collection *The Days After Always* (Shoestring Press, 2015).

'Down the Aisle', by Jo Brandon, was first published in her debut collection *The Learned Goose* (Valley Press, 2015).

'photographs from our holiday in bed', by Ali Lewis, was first published on *Ink, Sweat and Tears* in 2015.

'I Went to a Parthenogenesis Party and Met an Aphid', by James Horrocks, was previously published in *NowThen* 5 (2013).

'Auto-Pornographia', by Amy McCauley, was first published in *The Interpreter's House* 58, February 2015.

'Cigarettes', by George David Clark, was previously published in *The Yale Review* 101.4 (2013) and in his collection *Reveille* (University of Arkansas Press, 2015).

About the poets

Jamie Baxter grew up in Solihull and works in London, having graduated from Durham University where he studied Engineering. He has had poems published by *The Next Review, Astronaut* zine, *The Cadaverine* magazine and *Silkworms Ink*. He has also attended a Tower Poetry School.

Vasiliki Albedo Bennu was born in Greece and lived in London and New York before returning to Athens recently to take advantage of the local lucrative economic opportunities. Her poems have appeared in *The Interpreter's House, Ink, Sweat and Tears, Belleville Park Pages* and the US magazine *Beloit Poetry Journal*.

Nisha Bhakoo is a writer and video artist. Her poetry has appeared in *Poems in Which, Ink, Sweat and Tears, The Cadaverine* and *Morphrog*. In 2015, she was shortlisted for the Jane Martin Poetry Prize, won third prize in the Ledbury Festival competition and was selected for the GlogauAIR artist residency scheme in Berlin.

Julia Bird grew up in Gloucestershire and now lives in London. She works part-time for the Poetry School, and produces touring live literature shows as a freelancer. Her first collection *Hannah and the Monk* was published by Salt in 2008, and her second, *Twenty-Four Seven Blossom*, in 2013.

Sophia Blackwell was born in Newcastle in 1982. Her poetry has been anthologised by Bloodaxe, Nine Arches and Sidekick Books. She is the author of one poetry collection, *Into Temptation* (2009), and a novel, *After My Own Heart* (2012). Her second collection is due out in 2016 with Burning Eye Books.

Jo Brandon has a degree in Creative Writing from the University of Leeds and is former General Editor of *The Cadaverine*. Jo's pamphlet, *Phobia*, was published in 2012 and her collection *The Learned Goose* in 2015, both by Valley Press. She can be found online at www.jobrandon.com

Annie Brechin has been published in *The Wolf, Stand, Magma, Rising, B O D Y, Paris Lit Up* and others. In 2003 she was awarded a Jerwood/Arvon Young Poets Apprenticeship. She is a former Poetry Editor for *The Prague Revue* and moved from Paris to Dubai last year.

Alan Buckley's debut pamphlet *Shiver* (tall-lighthouse, 2009) was a Poetry Book Society Choice. His second pamphlet, *The Long Haul*, will be published by HappenStance in 2016. He works in Oxford as a psychotherapist, and as a school writer-in-residence for the charity First Story.

In a previous life, **Helen Clare** was a science teacher. She now works on projects which combine science, poetry and learning, including a poetry residency at the Museum of Science and Industry in Manchester. Her published work includes *Mollusc* (Comma, 2004) and *Entomology* (HappenStance, 2014).

George David Clark's *Reveille* won the Miller Williams Prize and his new work can be found or is forthcoming in *AGNI, The Believer, Blackbird, The Cincinnati Review, FIELD, Measure* and elsewhere. He edits the journal *32 Poems* and lives with his wife and their three young children in Washington, Pennsylvania.

Mel Denham lives in the literature-loving city of Melbourne. She's had a lifelong love affair with poetry but has only recently begun writing it. She is working on a collection of poems about her other love, the postal system. Brief musings on this and other ephemera can be found at meldenham.com

Isobel Dixon is the author of *Weather Eye, A Fold in the Map* and *The Tempest Prognosticator* and co-wrote and performed in *The Debris Field*. In 2016 Mariscat will publish a pamphlet, *The Leonids*, and Nine Arches will publish her new collection, *Bearings*.

Hugh Dunkerley grew up in Edinburgh and Bath and now lives in mildly erotic Brighton with his wife and young son. He has published one full collection, *Hare* (Cinnamon Press, 2010), in which sex and nature feature prominently. He is currently working on a new collection about fatherhood.

Victoria Gatehouse lives in Yorkshire. Her poems have appeared in magazines and anthologies including *Mslexia, Magma, The Rialto, The Interpreter's House, Prole* and *Furies*. Her competition wins and placements include Ilkley and *Mslexia*, and she is currently working on a first collection.

Mary Gilonne is a translator from Devon, who has lived in France for many years. She has won the 2015 Wenlock Prize and been shortlisted for the Bridport Prize (2010, 2011, 2015) and commended for the Teignmouth and Caterpillar Prizes (2015). She is working hopefully towards her first collection.

Stephanie Green has an MPhil in Creative Writing from Glasgow University. Her latest pamphlet is *Flout* (HappenStance, 2015). She is a Creative Writing tutor and also reviews Theatre and Dance. Originally London-based, she moved, via Wales, to Edinburgh in 2000. See http://sites.google.com/site/stephgreen1/home

Robert Hamberger was first prizewinner in Chroma's International Queer Writing Competition in 2006. His full-length collections include *The Smug Bridegroom* (Five Leaves, 2002) and *Torso* (Redbeck, 2007). His fourth collection, *Blue Wallpaper*, is forthcoming from Waterloo Press. He lives in Brighton.

Ramona Herdman is working on a pamphlet for publication by HappenStance in 2017. She was one of the Poetry Trust's Aldeburgh Eight in 2011. Lately, she is writing mostly about alcohol. She tweets occasionally @ramonaherdman

Hilaire has published short stories and poetry in British and Australian magazines and several anthologies. *Triptych Poets* 1 (Blemish Books, 2010) featured a selection of her poems. She is working on a poetry collection with Joolz Sparkes, *London Undercurrents*, unearthing women's voices north and south of the river.

Lynn Hoffman is a cook and a poet. He describes himself as a beer evangelist, spreading the good word of the good taste. He is author of *The Bachelor's Cat, bang-BANG, Radiation Days, The New Short Course in Wine, Short Course in Beer* and *Short Course in Rum*.

James Horrocks is a writer and musician living in Bolton and born in Salford. He recently completed a Masters in Creative Writing at the University of Manchester, specialising in poetry. His poems have been published in *The Manchester Anthology* 2014 and *Now Then* magazine.

Kirsten Irving co-runs Sidekick Books with Jon Stone and her own poetry has been published by HappenStance and Salt. She normally writes a lot about robots. And schoolgirls too. And sometimes cannibals. Sexy robot schoolgirl cannibals.

Victoria Kennefick's debut poetry pamphlet, *White Whale* (Southword Editions, 2015), won the Munster Literature Centre Fool for Poetry Chapbook Competition 2014 and the Saboteur Award for Best Poetry Pamphlet in 2015. Follow her @VKennefick

Amy Key was born in Dover and grew up in Kent and the North East. She now lives and works in London. She co-edits the online journal *Poems in Which*. Her pamphlet *Instead of Stars* was published by tall-lighthouse in 2009. Her debut collection *Luxe* was published by Salt in 2013.

Lancashire-born **Angela Kirby** lives in London but has spent time in France, Spain and America. She is the author of five books on food and gardening and her poems have been published widely. Her fourth poetry collection, *The Days After Always: New and Selected Poems*, was published by Shoestring Press in 2015.

Anja Konig grew up in the German language and now writes in English. Her first pamphlet, *Advice for an Only Child*, was short-listed for the Michael Marks Poetry Award in 2015. Its advantages are: 1) it is very cheap, 2) it is very short.

Ali Lewis has work forthcoming in *Brittle Star* and *Asterism*. He organises the arts night Theme and was runner-up in the Poetry Book Fair competition. He is currently collaborating with the contemporary classical music group The Hermes Experiment, and is studying for an MA in Creative Writing at Goldsmiths.

Holly Magill is a poet from Worcestershire. She has a BA in Creative Writing from University Of Birmingham and has had poems in various publications, including *Nutshells and Nuggets, The Stare's Nest* and *Three Drops & A Cauldron*. She is fond of cats and strong tea above most things.

Ikhda Ayuning Maharsi has worked in television, advertising and as a scriptwriter on a sitcom in Indonesia. She performed her poetry for the first time in 2011, at Cité Internationale Universitaire de Paris. Her debut pamphlet, *Ikhda, by Ikhda*, was published by the Emma Press in 2014. She lives in Tréguier, France.

Amy McCauley's poetry has been published widely in anthologies and magazines, including *The Poetry of Sex* (Penguin, 2014), *Hallelujah for 50ft Women* (Bloodaxe, 2015) and *Best British Poetry 2015* (Salt). She is a PhD candidate at Aberyswtyth University and Poetry Editor for *New Welsh Review*.

Laura McKee's poems have appeared in journals including *Other Poetry, Obsessed With Pipework* and *The Journal*. In 2015 she was nominated for Best Single Poem at the Forward Prizes, was a winner in the Guernsey International Poetry Competition, and was shortlisted for the Bridport Prize.

Fiona Moore lives in Greenwich. Her second pamphlet, *Night Letter*, was published by HappenStance in September 2015. She is assistant editor at *The Rialto* and blogs at *Displacement*.

Steve Nash is a writer, lecturer and terrible musician based in Yorkshire. He was named the 2014 Saboteur Spoken Word Performer of the Year and his first collection, *Taking the Long Way Home*, is available now from Stairwell Books.

Richard O'Brien's poems have featured in *Oxford Poetry* and *The Best British Poetry 2013*, and in 2015 he won the sonnet category of the London Book Fair Poetry Prize. His pamphlets include *The Emmores* (Emma Press, 2014) and *A Bloody Mess* (Valley Press, 2015). He is working on a PhD in contemporary verse drama.

Camille Ralphs started in Stoke, and has studied in Lancaster, Cambridge and now Oxford. She is a senior poetry editor at *The Missing Slate*, and was 2014's Cambridge editor-in-chief of *The Mays Anthology*. Her debut pamphlet, *Malkin*, was published by the Emma Press in 2015.

After graduating from Oxford in 2012, **Emma Reay** was a little lost. She tried a few different things but soon decided to give adult life the slip and hitchhike around America, where she may still be.

Kristen Roberts is a poet from Melbourne. Her poems have won several awards and have been published in *Award Winning Australian Writing, Quadrant, Australian Love Poems 2013* and *page seventeen*. Her first pamphlet, *The Held and the Lost*, was published in 2014 with the Emma Press.

Jacqueline Saphra's *The Kitchen of Lovely Contraptions* (flipped eye, 2011) was nominated for the Aldeburgh First Collection Prize. An illustrated book of prose poems, *If I Lay on my Back I Saw Nothing but Naked Women*, was published by the Emma Press in 2014 and won the Saboteur Award for Best Collaborative Work.

Lawrence Schimel was born in New York and has lived in Madrid, Spain, for over 17 years. He is the author of two poetry pamphlets in English – *Fairy Tales for Writers* and *Deleted Names* – and a full collection in Spanish, *Desayuno en la cama*, as well as a collection of erotic short stories, *His Tongue*.

Stephen Sexton lives in Belfast, where he is studying at the Seamus Heaney Centre for Poetry. His poems have appeared in *Poetry Ireland, Poetry London* and *Best British Poetry 2015*. His pamphlet, *Oils* (Emma Press, 2014), was the 2015 PBS Winter Pamphlet Choice.

Natalie Shaw lives and works in London. Her work has appeared in various print and online journals and anthologies, most recently *And Other Poems* and Paper Swan's *Schooldays*.

Di Slaney is a smallholder, marketing consultant and publisher from Nottinghamshire. She co-owns Candlestick Press, and her poems have been widely published. She won first prize in the 2014 Brittle Star and 2015 Four Corners poetry competitions. Her first full collection, *Reward for Winter,* is available from Valley Press.

Ruth Stacey is a writer, artist, librarian and tutor. Her debut collection, *Queen, Jewel, Mistress,* was published by Eyewear in 2015. Her pamphlet, *Fox Boy,* was published by Dancing Girl Press in 2014. She designs the covers for V. Press poetry pamphlets and lives in Worcestershire.

Jon Stone was born in Derby and is currently London-based. His collection, *School of Forgery,* was a Poetry Book Society Recommendation and he won an Eric Gregory Award in 2012. He's also co-creator of Sidekick Books (www.drfulminare.com), publishers of collaborative creative anthologies.

Kelley Swain is a writer and editor based in London. She is the author of several books of poetry, a novel, and a forthcoming memoir – *The Naked Muse* (Valley Press) – as well as a contributor to *The Lancet.* Kelley is a member of the Nevada Street Poets.

Ali Thurm was born in Tynemouth and brought up in the north of England. She now lives in London with her three children. She teaches, writes poetry and short stories, and is working on a novel, *The Quiet Water Spy.*

Sara-Mae Tuson is a freelance editor and copywriter. She has had short fiction, poetry and articles published in a wide range of publications, including the Salt anthology *Overheard, Scouting* magazine, *Ink, Sweat and Tears, Obsessed with Pipework, 433, Trespass, The London Magazine, Inky Needles, Rising* and more.

Nicola Warwick was born in Kent and now lives in Suffolk, where she works in local government. Her first collection, *Groundings,* was published by Cinnamon Press in 2014.

Ruth Wiggins lives in London. Her work has appeared in UK magazines and anthologies, and has been commended in recent competitions. Her first pamphlet, *Myrtle,* was published in 2014 by the Emma Press. Her photography book, *Wonder Women of America*, was published in 2008.

Jerrold Yam (b. 1991) is the Singaporean author of three poetry collections: *Intruder* (2014), *Scattered Vertebrae* (2013) and *Chasing Curtained Suns* (2012). He has received awards from the British Council, National University of Singapore and Poetry Book Society, and been nominated for the Forward and Pushcart Prizes.

About the editors

Rachel Piercey is a former editor at *The Cadaverine* magazine and a current editor at the Emma Press. She studied English Literature at St Hugh's College, Oxford, where she won the Newdigate Prize in 2008. Her illustrated pamphlet of love poems, *The Flower and the Plough*, was published by the Emma Press 2013 and her second pamphlet, *Rivers Wanted*, in 2014.

Emma Wright studied Classics at Brasenose College, Oxford. She worked in ebook production at Orion Publishing Group before leaving to set up the Emma Press in 2012. In 2015 she toured the UK with the Myths and Monsters poetry tour for children, supported with funding from Arts Council England as part of the Lottery-funded Grants for the Arts programme. She lives in Birmingham.

THE EMMA PRESS

small press, big dreams

The Emma Press is an independent publisher dedicated to producing beautiful, thought-provoking books. It was founded in 2012 by Emma Wright in Winnersh, UK, and is now based in Birmingham. It was shortlisted for the Michael Marks Award for Poetry Pamphlet Publishers in both 2014 and 2015.

In 2015 we travelled around the country with Myths and Monsters, a tour of poetry readings and workshops aimed at children aged 9-12. This was made possible with a grant from Grants for the Arts, supported using public funding by the National Lottery through Arts Council England.

Our current publishing programme features a mixture of themed poetry anthologies and single-author poetry and prose pamphlets, with an ongoing engagement with the works of the Roman poet Ovid. We publish books which excite us and we are often on the lookout for new writing.

Sign up to the monthly Emma Press newsletter to hear about our events, publications and upcoming calls for submissions. All of our books are available to buy from our online shop, as well as to order or buy from all good bookshops.

http://theemmapress.com
http://emmavalleypress.blogspot.co.uk/

Also from the Emma Press

A POETIC PRIMER FOR LOVE AND SEDUCTION

Edited by Rachel Piercey and Emma Wright

Series: The Emma Press Ovid

RRP £10 / ISBN 978-0-9574596-3-2

An anthology of instructional poems by modern poets dispensing advice on love, seduction, relationships and heartbreak, channelling the spirit of Roman poet Ovid.

THE EMMORES, by Richard O'Brien

Series: The Emma Press Picks

RRP £5 / ISBN 978-0-9574596-4-9

Richard O'Brien deploys every trick in the love poet's book in this irresistible mix of tender odes, introspective sonnets, exuberant free verse and anthems of sexual persuasion.

MYRTLE, by Ruth Wiggins

With an introduction by Deryn Rees-Jones
RRP £6.50 / ISBN 978-1-910139-05-9

In her debut pamphlet *Myrtle*, Ruth Wiggins celebrates the
primal forces of nature and the human heart. Interweaving the
ancient with the modern world, she explores fertility and death,
in poems that are imbued with a subtle eroticism.

AWOL

By John Fuller and Andrew Wynn Owen,
with colour illustrations by Emma Wright
Series: Art Squares
RRP £12.50 / ISBN 978-1-910139-28-8

In rural Wales, John Fuller has composed a letter on the subject of
travel: warning against it, and wondering about people's presences
and absences. Andrew Wynn Owen replies with enthusiasm,
matching John's poetic form while hopping from gallery to garret.

MALKIN, by Camille Ralphs

Series: The Emma Press Picks

RRP £5 / ISBN 978-1-910139-30-1

Malkin brims and bubbles with the voices of those accused in the Pendle Witch Trials of 1612. Thirteen men and women – speaking across the centuries via Ralphs' heady use of free spelling – plead, boast and confess, immersing the reader in this charged and dangerous time in history.

TRUE TALES OF THE COUNTRYSIDE, by Deborah Alma

With an introduction by Helen Ivory

RRP £6.50 / ISBN 978-1-910139-26-4

Deborah Alma writes vividly about sex, love and ageing in rural Shropshire and Wales, reflecting on her experiences as a mixed-race, British-Asian woman. Eyeballs pop, fresh piss steams and women come – loudly – in poems which startle with their honesty.

BEST FRIENDS FOREVER: POEMS ABOUT FEMALE
FRIENDSHIP, edited by Amy Key
RRP £10 / ISBN 978-1-910139-07-3

The idea of the best friend defines the social and emotional lives of
many young girls and continues to have an impact into adulthood,
even as The One BFF relaxes into many close female friendships.
Best Friends Forever is a celebration of the transformative power of
this frequently overlooked and misunderstood relationship.

IF I LAY ON MY BACK I SAW NOTHING BUT NAKED WOMEN

By Jacqueline Saphra, with colour illustrations by Mark Webber
Series: Art Squares
RRP £12.50 / ISBN 978-1-910139-06-6

A sumptuous sequence of prose poems about the eccentric activi-
ties of parents and step-parents, as seen from a child's perspective.
The poems are illustrated with linocuts which celebrate real bodies
and complement the vivid atmosphere.